FROM THE ISLANDS

Edited by Allison Dowse

First published in Great Britain in 2000 by
YOUNG WRITERS
Remus House,
Coltsfoot Drive,
Woodston,
Peterborough, PE2 9JX
Telephone (01733) 890066

HB ISBN 0 75431 926 1
SB ISBN 0 75431 927 X

FOREWORD

This year, the Young Writers' Future Voices competition proudly presents a showcase of the best poetic talent from over 42,000 up-and-coming writers nationwide.

Successful in continuing our aim of promoting writing and creativity in children, our regional anthologies give a vivid insight into the thoughts, emotions and experiences of today's younger generation, displaying their inventive writing in its originality.

The thought, effort, imagination and hard work put into each poem impressed us all and again the task of editing proved challenging due to the quality of entries received, but was nevertheless enjoyable. We hope you are as pleased as we are with the final selection and that you continue to enjoy *Future Voices From The Islands* for many years to come.

To Nana, Aunty Helen, Tom, Pat,
Uncle David, Uncle Kieron, Aunty
Catherine, Johnathon, Anna, and James,

HOPE YOU ENJOY THIS
BOOK!
Andrew xxx

To Jean ... with love, ...

... Laura Lucas Karen Family

Catherine, Johnathan, Jane and James

Hope you Enjoy this
Book!

xxx

CONTENTS

Donna Whalley	36
Georgina Pryke	38
David Orders	39
Sarah King	40
Saha Ibrahim	41
Michelle Draper	42
Eva Corcoran	43
Stephanie Groom	44
Luke Simpson	45
Rachel Grainger	46
Jamie Smith	47
Stephanie Woods	48
Vicky Radcliffe	49
Adam Bingham	50
Katherine Hicks	51
Barry Maddrell	52
Michelle McBride	53
John Myers	54
David Mercer	55
Kerrie McCauley	56
Christina Davidson	57
Alice Armstrong	58
William Bollen	59

Brae High School

Lindsay Clark	60
David Odie	61
Michael Manson	62
Ross Smith	63
Nikita Johnson	64
Rachael Blyth	65
Terry Balfour	66
Kirsty Thomason	67
Stuart Milne	68
Jason Mayes	70
Sarah Hargreaves	71
Diana Mowat	72
Angela Murray	73

Christopher Cope	74
Stephen Rocks	75
Nicholas Davidson	76
Jenna Johnson	77
Peter Robertson	78

De La Salle College

Vincent McAviney	79
Brendan Roberts	80
Sean Kenny	81
Jonathan Poole	82
Rory Harman	83
James Warley	84
Tom Whiteley	85
David Gaffney	86
Declan Varian	87
Jason Olver	88
Luke Palmer	89
Harley Woodward	90
Edward Cookson	91
Nicholas Hogan	92
Hugh Thomas	93
Neil Cotillard	94
Paul Williams	95

Mid Yell Junior High School

Brian Henderson	96
Marcus Nisbet	97
Matthew Simpson	98
Brendan Scollay	99
Martha Clark	100
Hayley Nisbet	101
Vincent Tonner	102
Mark Odie	103
Lee Jamieson	104
Carly Gray	105
Belinda Anderson	106

The Poems

DADDY

He is my day
He is my night
He is my forever redeeming light!
He is my what
  My who
  My when
  My where
I know he said that he'd always be there
He will always be deep within my heart
I know with his love, we'll never part
With his hands, my heart he'll mend
Because I know now, he is my only true
  Friend!
People say to me
'It's OK, it'll be fine!'
But there are sorrows you can't
  Wash away with wine!
Love is deeper than valleys
And higher than any mountain,
  So I'm *told!*
But I wish he was there for me
  Just to *hold!*

He's in a higher place
  Somewhere that I can't
  Touch or feel his face
But I know now, anywhere I go I see him,
Because he is here within the human race!

My family is getting smaller every day
I wish that I can hear him one more time, say
  'It's OK! *Daddy's here!'*

Linda C Baird (17)

CHRISTMAS MORNING

Santa works very hard all year
To bring us a little Christmas cheer.
He slaves away all night and day
So all the children can wake up to play.
Sacks and sacks of toys he makes
He even sometimes bakes some cakes.
As the twenty-fifth draws near
The whole world starts to smile and cheer.
Santa's sleigh is clean and sparkly
Even Rudolph is acting larky.
When the sleigh is piled up high
It is time for Rudolph to take to the sky.
As the snow begins to fall,
It's time for Santa to make that call.
From house to house
He swoops and flies.
Down the chimneys to leave a surprise
And so that morning when the children awake
A very loud noise they start to make.
They race downstairs all bleary eyed
To see what Santa's left behind.
With bulging stockings over the fireplace
Their little hearts begin to race.
They open their gifts, they shout and scream
Surely this must be a dream,
Or maybe Santa's really been.

Monique Bush (14)

DEMON RAISER

The wizard sat upon a hill,
Gathering in his mighty will.
The air around him crackled and sparked
And the floor around him became marked,
With mystical, strong symbols.

He touched the ground,
With his skull headed staff
And in a terrible voice he shouted;
'Rise up and be my slave!'
And the air before him shimmered
And a demon appeared.

It was an awful beast, with two clawed feet
And hideous fangs and green scaly skin.
Then the wizard commanded
'Hunt me some food,
Get me oxen, meat by the load!'

When the monster returned,
The great wizard said,
'Be gone!'
And the creature went home.

Daniel James (12)
Ballakermeen High School

SCHOOL

Everyone looks forward for the dinner bell to go,
They're looking outside, through the windows' glass
And moaning for their homework to show,
But finally the teacher lets us free from the tedious class.

The next day's just the same,
Writing pages and pages in our book.
There's never any time for a game,
The teachers yell, as the kids give funny looks.

When you think the work is complete,
You pack your things away
And get ready to go and have something to eat,
'Wait! The lesson's not finished yet,' is what the teacher will say.

> Work, work,
> No play,
> What day is it today?
> *Friday!*
> Ding-a-ling-a-ling,
> There's the bell,
> Let's go,
> But then the teacher had to go and yell,
> 'Wait! Here's your homework.'
> Homework, homework,
> We get it every day,
> We never get a break away,
> Boring maths homework,
> I'll never get it done,
> Sums, sums,
> There's never any fun.

Now's the afternoon
And I'm sitting in my room,
Doing my homework,
At half past three,
When I could be watching TV.

Dawn Winn (12)
Ballakermeen High School

MAGIC

If I was a magician I would say . . .

Hocus pocus pudding and pie
Give me wings and I can fly.
Jump up and down, move it all around
Give me the speed to run along the ground.

I want the power to eat any food
I wish I could stop people from being crude.
I wish all my clothes were named Nike
And I wish I had a skilfully skilful bike.

I wish I had the money to buy a big house
I wish I could give cheese to every little mouse
I wish everyone was kind and nice
And I wish lots of people liked curry and rice

And finally I wish for Euro 2000 that
England would win,
But usually the Germans throw it
Straight in the bin.

Robbie Ward (12)
Ballakermeen High School

WITCH'S BREW

Double, double toil and trouble,
Fire burn and cauldron bubble
Broth we will make to take the world
Toe of a croc that had been curled.

Double, double toil and trouble,
Fire burn and cauldron bubble
Just watch your mummy,
'Cause soon she'll be in my tummy.

Double, double toil and trouble,
Fire burn and cauldron bubble
Leg of dog, mud from a bog
The moon may shiver, it will make you quiver,

Double, double toil and trouble,
Fire burn and cauldron bubble.

Amy Clarke (12)
Ballakermeen High School

IF I WAS A MAGICIAN

Magic, magic everywhere!
From head to toe and in the air
Here I am standing near
The magic buzzing past my ear.
You can't see it
But ya can feel it

Sparkle and whiz
And whiz and sparkle
I'm a magician
Always feeling a tingle
When I want to fly around
I hear a really loud sound.

What's that I feel, magic in the air
I take a long good stare.
But there's nothing there
Ahh! I'm lifting from the ground
Without any sound
I see the stars glistening in my eyes

My magic starts to sigh
What should I do now.
I take a look around
And hear a strange sound
Oh! my goodness
I'm lifting from the ground

I face the sun
And then drop down
My heart beating fast
I now have done my task
I'm a real magician now!

Leanda Clark (12)
Ballakermeen High School

POLLUTION

Pollution is a very bad thing,
For middle class to the king,
In the morning, all that smog,
Replaces our normal fog.
It doesn't help our breathing,
It leaves us all seething,
'Why put up with this?' we ask,
Soon we'll have to wear a mask,
Just to get round our town.
To this we answer with a frown,
'How can our world be better?'
Asked a man, who was considerably wetter,
Because he'd come through the rain,
Which was turning into a pain,
As the acid in it, is starting to become,
A real enemy for some.
Washing lead off our roofs,
Hurting our animals' hooves.
We say to him 'Stop using cars!'
Or the world will be like Mars,
Try using bikes,
Or going on hikes,
Stop being bitter
And dumping litter,
Into the earth,
With silent mirth,
So come on and do your bit,
To help the Earth before we kill it!

Robert Crellin (13)
Ballakermeen High School

HALLOWE'EN NIGHT

I always look forward to Hallowe'en night,
When devils and witches give you a fright,
Dressed up in costumes with painted faces,
Candy like chocolates and liquorice laces.

Pumpkins are cut out, hollowed and lit,
When you go trick or treating you get quite a bit,
Bobbing apples is one thing we do,
But why Hallowe'en's celebrated I haven't a clue!

But when it's all over we feel a bit sad,
But the sweets and the money are not all that bad!
It comes to November but never fear
Hallowe'en night will be back next year.

Hayley Rourke (12)
Ballakermeen High School

SCHOOL IS ACE

School is ace,
If you know what I mean,
It's better than chocolate,
But not ice-cream.

Most of the teachers,
Are alright,
But some of the teachers.
I dislike.

My favourite subject,
Has to be PE,
My worst subject,
Is geography.

I'm not very good,
At IT,
I'm much better,
At history.

School is ace,
If you know what I mean,
It's better than chocolate,
But not ice-cream.

Michael Corlett (12)
Ballakermeen High School

GHOSTS

Growling, howling that's all they do,
They scare the lives out of me and you.
They hang around all night long,
Getting ready to bite your tongue.
In the morning they go away
And stay away for a whole day.
But if they ever saw the light,
It would give them such a fright.
So if you don't like them hanging around,
Close your eyes and lie on the ground.
Even though they fly in the air,
They don't even seem to care.
If you die you might become one,
So make sure all your business is done.
They have cousins as scary as them,
Maybe even a really big hen.
If you go to the haunted house,
You may get frightened by a mouse.
So next time you are messing around,
Don't forget to listen for the sound,
Of howling, growling ghostly ghosts,
Who might come out and fry you to toast.

Eilis Kerford (12)
Ballakermeen High School

IF I WAS A MAGICIAN

Hocus pocus turn around
and put your hands to the ground
Take one step left and one step right
give me the power to boogie all night
I wish I could be a professional footballer
and always be the best scorer
I wish I could take one step, two steps and leap up into the sky
and then I would begin to fly
I would be a skilful bike
and turn into anything I like
Any person that annoyed me
I would turn them into a flea.

Michael Peace (12)
Ballakermeen High School

MAGIC!

As I walked out the door, a sight met my eyes,
The grass had turned purple and as for the skies,
They were a deep yellow, rich as a lemon,
For a moment, 'Cor blimey!' I think I saw heaven.
As I walked along the granite, grey road,
I saw an elephant being devoured by a toad,
Rubbing my eyes I carried on walking,
But then I saw two penguins talking.
I shook my head and carried on,
Then I saw a strange blue sun,
But it was not up in the sky,
It was being pushed along by a dragonfly,
A dragonfly that had no wings,
Instead it had some other things,
A pair of wheels and human hands,
Its tail was wrapped in rubber bands.
I let it pass on its way,
Strangely it stopped by to say,
'Yo man, save the trees, hey-hey,'
and 'get your licence now, or pay.'
It carried on pushing its sun down the road,
Flattening the hungry toad.
As I looked across the bog,
I saw my mum feeding a frog,
I ran up to her and asked her why,
She was in this strange world I had come by.
She stared at me and looked quite tragic,
'Son, I did it all by magic!'

Thomas Iain Dixon (12)
Ballakermeen High School

IF I WAS A MAGICIAN

If I was a magician,
I would cast spells and use a wand
Kazaam, bang, wallop!

If I was a magician,
I would turn my enemies into frogs
And give my friends magic purses
Which always made money,
Kazaam, bang, wallop!

If I was a magician,
I would stop poverty in the world
And stop wars,
Kazaam, bang, wallop!

If I was a magician,
I would make wishing potions
And give them to my family
Kazaam, bang, wallop!

If I was a magician,
I would make my brother disappear
            Poof!

Sarah Smart (12)
Ballakermeen High School

THE COOL COUNTRYSIDE

In the spring the grass is sweet,
The birds are twittering next to the fields of wheat,
The postman waves as he rides past on his bike,
It's the sound of the trickling river I like,
Then there's the odd rabbit nibbling on grass verges,
The bell of the old chapels and the churches,
The smell of the garlic and sweet elderflower,
What ruins it is the smell of cows' muck, it's sour!
I hear the sheep baaing, the horses and cattle,
The horses' hooves going tittle-tat-tattle.
A gentle breeze,
Puts everything at ease,
Everyone suits the country,
Like a koala in a gum tree.

Paula Carse (12)
Ballakermeen High School

DIABLO: LORD OF TERROR

As darkness falls I become afraid
Of the evil that lurks in the night.
I wish someone would seek out this evil
And destroy it once and for all!

This Lord of Terror has escaped free
Seeking for helpless souls to consume.
He placed himself inside a desecrated cathedral
Where an innocent town called Tristram lies.

As Diablo stalks the aisles of the cathedral
There are unearthly cries in the dead of the night.
The shrieks sound like people
Crying out in pain and terror!

Oh, who could imagine this horror?
Everyone is afraid of the terrors underneath.
They all wait in their homes
For the apocalypse that will soon come . . .

Alexander Yiu (12)
Ballakermeen High School

OCEAN

As I stepped into the cool calm waters,
I could see a different world.
With colour and glamour and rocks everywhere,
Flounders and starfish all hidden away in the sand.

I kept swimming and seeing great bottle-nosed dolphins
Jumping and gliding along.
This was totally a different world to the dark,
Polluted land that I and everyone else live on.

But out of the corner of my eye I saw . . . black!
There were dead fish floating at the surface,
Then I realised what it was, when I saw an oil tanker
Lodged on some rocks, oil seeping out of it.

Then I saw a school of fish caught in a fishing net,
A turtle with them, I saw some men lift them onto the boat.
Then they threw the turtle back dead!
I thought we are destroying this world too.

David Dawson (12)
Ballakermeen High School

TEACHER'S PET

Teacher's pet is not pretty,
Not clever, intelligent, nice or witty.
Every break she takes him out,
Until she heard a frightful shout!

You see, when we're naughty
She won't let us have a look.
So we ran into the classroom -
And shut it in a book!

It had seemed like months had passed,
Waiting for the bell to blast.
Soon it did and we went home,
I heard the pet moan and groan!

That night I made it a bed
I woke up that morning
And found it dead!

I got ready for school
And tried to act cool
I had another look at the pet
As I screamed
I shook the house

I could not believe it was a
Mouse!

Jessica Rhiannon Ainsley (12)
Ballakermeen High School

MY BEST MATE EMMA!

Emma Skillen is her name,
being nice is her game.
Laughing all day long,
while singing a song.

She likes dancing at the cave,
while dancing she gives me a wave.
She is such an ace best mate,
I would never give her hate.

She is loud, funny and mad,
she is never ever sad.
Her blue eyes are so bright,
they sparkle all the time at night.

She likes going down town every week
and playing hide and seek.
She lives round the corner from me,
I always go round and have some tea.

She likes eating chocolate lots,
but she doesn't eat it when it rots.
She is nowhere near fat,
she will never be that.

She has long brown hair,
she is mental when we give her dares.
She is mental and daring,
that's why I like my best mate Emma.

Elle Townsend (12)
Ballakermeen High School

THREE LITTLE TEDDY BEARS

T hree little teddies sitting on my shelf,
H ow I love to hug them tight
E ven when I'm old.

T hen I see that lovely one
E ven though he's torn
D irty and ragged,
D usty and worn.
Y ellow and brown fur and a

B lack button nose.
E very time I look at him
A little whisper says
R emember not to leave me here, bring me up to bed.

Charlotte Copparelli (13)
Ballakermeen High School

A MATE CALLED LINZI

I have a special mate
and Linzi is her name
she is really kind
I am mad but she does not care
she has beautiful dark hair.

Her eyes sparkle in the sun
she is so much fun!
On Fridays we go to the cave
it is like a rave.

My mate Linzi is round the bend
and totally mental
she kicks and screams
and bawls and shouts
but I know my friend
she's round the bend
and marvellously mental!

She's beautiful and she's pretty
her name is Linzi Kelly
and she is smelly, of flowers
and once again her name is
Linzi Kelly!

Julia Featherstone (12)
Ballakermeen High School

SWANSEA FC ARE THE BEST!

Even though they're division three,
They're still my favourite, *Swansea FC!*
Losing just about every match,
When they play good they get the catch!

Beating their worst enemy *Cardiff AFC,*
That is one thing I'd like to see!
Beat them 4-0, 5-0 I don't care,
Just beat them here and beat them there!

The Swansea fans are very wise,
While the Cardiff fans we despise!
People think Jason Price is hot,
While Roger Freestone saves a Cardiff shot!

If we could beat Man United,
I would be dead excited!
Even though that'll never be,
We can still dream, can't we?

Gregory John Hutchinson (13)
Ballakermeen High School

THEY ARE COMING TO GET YOU!

Hallowe'en is coming, ha, ha, ha,
Hallowe'en is coming, ha, ha, ha.
All the kids that trick or treat,
To get all the candy sweets.
All the pumpkins glowing bright,
The kids in costumes will give you a fright.

Hallowe'en is here, hee, hee, hee,
Hallowe'en is here, hee, hee, hee.
Haunted houses come alive,
All the ghosts are in the sky.
All the cobwebs in the house,
Scaring off the little mouse.

Hallowe'en is coming, ha, ha, ha,
Hallowe'en is coming, ha, ha, ha.
Witches with their black cats,
Jumping out on giant rats.
All the broomsticks in a line,
All the witches popping wine.

Hallowe'en is here, hee, hee, hee,
Hallowe'en is here, hee, hee, hee.
Hallowe'en parties are fun,
Apart from your disturbing mum.
All the vampires blood to drink,
Bobbing apples in the sink.

Hallowe'en is over, ha, ha, ha,
Hallowe'en is over, hee, hee, hee,
All the kids in bed resting their little heads.

David Williams (12)
Ballakermeen High School

MY BEST FRIEND

My best mate,
She is fun,
She is great,
Her nickname is Wheils
I can't tell you why,
It's a best friend thing.

She is not at all sane,
She is totally round the bend.
But I don't care
She has golden blonde hair
With gorgeous blue eyes.

She fancies * * * * *
But that is a secret
I will not tell.

My best friend is great
We will be friends forever.

She is
Julia.

Linzi Kelly (12)
Ballakermeen High School

THE BUTTERFLY

T   actful and wonderful,
H   appy and colourful,
E   legant and pretty.

B   eautiful and witty,
U   tterly fantastic,
T   hough quite frantic.
T   ruly swift,
E   xtremely gifted,
R   adiant and busy,
F   luttering and dizzy.
L   iterally perfect,
Y   ummy to look at.

Jodie Teare (12)
Ballakermeen High School

MY IDEAL SCHOOL DAY!

My ideal school day would start at ten
Waking up in bed with bacon and egg;
Arriving at school in my fifty foot limo
Watching all the people they look a bit grimo.

Maths, science and then English
All these lessons are very childish;
I like PE now, Mr Teare is the best
Teaching athletics to me and all the rest.

My ideal school day would end at one
Finishing off the day with a very good bun;
Arriving at home in my fifty foot limo
Glancing at my mother she looks at bit grimo.

Maths, science and then English
All these lessons are very childish;
I like PE now, Mr Teare is the best
Teaching athletics to me and all the rest.

My real school day starts at nine
At one o'clock we're in the line
At two o'clock we're ready to dine
At three o'clock I'll finish this rhyme.

Samuel Cannell (12)
Ballakermeen High School

My Big Race

My legs are shaking,
My tummy rumbling,
My heart is breaking,
My hope
       Tumbling,

It's the final of the 800m
And I'm in it! Me!
My PB two minutes forty,
I thought I'll be quite hearty,
I'll put my tactics to the test,
(I hope I'll be better than all the rest),

The shot putt is on, the javelin postponed,
I wish I was being stoned,

The gun *goes* . . .
My spirit
      blows . . .

I run and run and *run* . . .

The rest is a blur,
Nothing seemed to occur,

In those two minutes,
(Such time passes so quick),

I cross the line
And the race doesn't end in a whine,

But cheers and claps,
I'm happy, I've completed two laps,

The race was a success
And I've got a new personal best,

Two minutes thirty-seven,
A gift from heaven.

Andrew Duncan (13)
Ballakermeen High School

TIM THE SPIDER

My pet lives in a matchbox,
He is very small you see.
He hardly ever shows his face,
But he comes out just for me.

I'll take him out for show and tell,
But nobody will see him.
They will all try to name my pet,
But I know his name is Tim.

When I went to school and in my class
They all said that he was cool,
But when I opened my matchbox,
He jumped out and went into the school.

When everybody saw him,
He gave them such a fright.
You see Tim is a spider
And does not like daylight.

Charlotte Cracknell (12)
Ballakermeen High School

LOCK THE DOORS, IT'S HALLOWE'EN!

Hallowe'en is great,
You sing hop-tu-naa,
The nice people give you money,
Then you run away.

Naughty children running around,
Having lots of fun,
Walking round with bags of sweets,
Playing knock a door run!

Children walking with their lanterns,
Ghosts and witches everywhere,
People playing prank phone calls,
You'd better be aware.

Throwing things at houses,
Mud bombs, eggs and spoons,
People shouting out their windows,
'Get lost you little goons.'

Ryan Chinn (12)
Ballakermeen High School

SCHOOL DAY

Monday morning I'm out of bed,
Nine o'clock, I'm turning red.

Foreign languages, I'm nodding off,
Half way through, I form a cough.

Break time comes, I feel alright,
Next lesson, makes me bite.

Lunchtime bell, all is well,
Now it's over, I'm in hell.

A double lesson, a living nightmare,
Oh Lord, me, can't you spare.

The bell has gone, time to go home.
A soak in the bath, bubbles of foam.

Bedtime now, I try to sleep,
The thoughts of school, I must keep.

I dread the morning,
Hold onto the dawning.

Helen Nicole Cowin (12)
Ballakermeen High School

WITCHES AND DEVILS

Witches are ugly and green,
With broomsticks and cats
And large pointy hats,
Everyone wants to scream!

The devil is the leader in red,
You know the one with horns on his head,
His trident is a long red stick,
Watch out or you'll get pricked!

Witches and devils are mean,
They come out every Hallowe'en,
What more could they want,
With a trident and broomstick,
They sure are ugly and mean!

Jenna Fozard (13)
Ballakermeen High School

SEA IN THE SUMMER

The sun wakes up, the sea turns blue,
The water sparkles gold and true.
The night has gone and the sky is clear,
The sun heats up and the crowds appear!

The waves lap softly on the sand below,
While the kids, they scream just saying hello.
As I wander along on the luscious green grass
I look down below on people swimming at last!

The sun is setting, as eve draws near
And I watch now sad, as the crowds disappear.
The sky turns orange, rose and pink,
But on this fair isle, night's here, black as ink!

A ship comes in, while the moon gives light,
The sky ever flawless, so the stars shine bright!
The heat of the day seems now long ago,
Though the sea still laps on the sand below!

Suzanna Power (12)
Ballakermeen High School

IF I WAS A MAGICIAN

Merlin,
Who was he?
Oh yes he was a magician
Just like me!

I'm better than any old wizards,
They're just total blizzards.
They're always getting muddled up
And doing experiments with tea cups.

Witches and warlocks,
They're the worst.
Mess with them,
They'll put you in a curse!

Of course, how could we forget the sorcerer of the world?
He's brave and brainy, but fights like a girl!

Fortune tellers, they think they're posh,
They'll tell you anything for a bit of dosh!
They tell you the future, oh wow
But if I put a spell on them I would make them bow.

Then there's me, a naughty magician,
Who would do anything for a competition.
Witches, warlocks, sorcerers and fortune tellers are all very well,
But me, I'm the fire burning from hell!

Joanne Hollows (12)
Ballakermeen High School

A HEAD WITH TWO FACES

I look in the mirror,
What do I see,
A young saddened face looking back at me.

The eyes deep
And somehow black,
Lines etched under eyes, just like a map.

The skin looks slightly grey,
But still youthful and clean,
Contradictory images, what can they mean?

Full pouting lips,
But no happy smile,
Just frowning marks that seem to go on for a mile.

Fashionable hairstyle,
Still, it's silvery grey,
A lock creeping forward, not in the way.

A pert little chin,
Pointed like the edge of a dice,
Hardened, never doubled, ever so precise.

The nose bony and narrow,
The nostrils flare wide,
Entices you forward to want to look inside.

The mind seems mysterious,
Something hidden in there?
I'm compelled to delve deeper, that's if I dare.

The picture becomes clearer,
As the story commences to enfold,
I'm seeing the face as an ancient, but familiar mould.

The young face is the grandchild,
Her nanna has gone,
But in Donna's face, her legend lives on.

Donna Whalley (15)
Ballakermeen High School

To Winter

Winter has crept upon us again,
Close on the heels of the autumn leaves.
He has covered our garden,
With a soft, white blanket
And snapped the flowers,
With his icy fingers.

He floats around silently,
Leaving no place untouched.
His long white hair and frosty beard,
His big, black boots and woollen coat.
Long icicles hang from his pointed nose
And his breath forms an icy cloud.

Winter draws swirling patterns,
On the frosted windows.
He leaves his artistic touch,
Right where we can see it,
But we only tend to notice,
The harm and grief he causes.

Each night he tampers with the car,
So it won't start again.
He leaves ice where we can't see it
And freezes up the water pipes.
Oh, how I wish winter would go away
And leave us with spring.

Georgina Pryke (13)
Ballakermeen High School

MY MAGIC POEM

On a dark, dark night I gave them all a fright
I sat on a hill and with all my will,
I cast a powerful spell
And brought forth hell.
I said 'Let Daniel be a pie' and gave a huge sigh
I gathered all my strength
And with my cauldron at an arm's length,
I cast again and threw in a weed
'Let Damian be a rabbit/beaver crossbreed
And let Jamie the mess, be a large pink dress.'
I needed all my power, I wanted everyone to cower,
I threw in a rotten stick and an old candle wick.
They went in with care and I threw my arms into the air
And let everyone who are wimps be big hairy shrimps
And clouds gathered in the sky, up so very high.
Lightning struck the steaming pot, it became so very hot.
It burst into flames and gave me pains.
I collapsed on the floor and then I saw
Daniel the pie, who said 'Hi.'
Damian the rabbit/beaver crossbreed who was a weed,
Jamie the dress, who still was a mess.

Pleased with the day, I went on my way,
I went home all alone,
I turned off the light with all my might,
I rested my sleepy head on a nice soft bed.

David Orders (12)
Ballakermeen High School

THE POEM I COULDN'T WRITE

I find that poems are hard to write
Even though I try with all my might
I get to the third line with no idea at all
I just wish I'd die and through the ground I hope to fall
If I think of an idea nothing will rhyme
I just sit there thinking 'An idea will come in time'
Suddenly an idea comes into my brain
Then I say thank you, thank you again
Thoughts start rushing all around my head
If I get any more I might just be dead
Then I write something about Hallowe'en
But what rhymes with Hallowe'en? Seen, bean, green
I decide to choose subjects with more rhyming words
Like something about snowmen, hippies or birds.
I spend my time thinking like at the beginning
When I started to write this poem so annoying
But now I think it's a total bummer
Writing this poem when I wish it was summer
Now the end of the lesson is drawing near
I wait in my seat shaking with fear
As my teacher draws closer with a look on his face
His shoe is undone. Don't trip over your lace
He tripped over a chair his wig flew up in the air
Everyone went 'Oh' but they didn't care.

Sarah King (13)
Ballakermeen High School

HALLOWE'EN

Hallowe'en's a great time of year,
Definitely no time of fear,
But for little kids, scared they might be so
But not for us teens no, no, no!
Witches, devils, ghosts and ghouls
And knock a'door runners and other fools.
Candy and chocolate, lollies and money,
All this for nothing it's really kinda funny.
Porches lit up with pumpkins and skeletons
All this trouble, to scare us and the little ones
Dressed up in costumes, everything including mummies
But as a reward we get candy to fill our tummies.
But Hallowe'en's not all about sweets,
It's not all about getting treats,
Because Hallowe'en normally ends
With us surrounded by families and friends,
Because without them we wouldn't have such a good time
And without them I wouldn't have got this good rhyme!

Sana Ibrahim (12)
Ballakermeen High School

SPORT

There are many types of sport today
For many, many people to play,
Running around the red, red track
What about rounders to give the ball a whack.

Some people might like to go to the gym,
Others may enjoy a relaxing swim.
Some people do really love sport
But some have not yet given any thought.

Sport is great when out in the sun,
But you do get hot when doing a run.
There really is lots of choice for you,
Lots and lots for me and you to do.

What about football, what about cricket?
You'll get caught out if you hit the wicket.
What about squash one against one
Or cross-country but that's very long.

When running tie your laces tight
Or you'll fall and it will give you a fright.
So come on try it, give it a go,
It's better than watching Tinky Winky, Dipsy, Laa Laa and Po.

Michelle Draper (12)
Ballakermeen High School

MY FIRST DAY AT SCHOOL

On my first day of school I was frightened, I was scared.
I had heard all the stories but my mother never cared.
I told her all the tales that my brother told to me.
She said, 'They all tell those stories, they're not true, you'll see.'
I went to bed that night, dreading the next day,
How could I not go to school, there wasn't any way.
I was dropped to school and left in the yard,
I'd have to hold tight and pretend to be hard.
Just then the bell went, it was time for school to start,
I was frightened, I was scared, I could even hear my heart.
But now that I am older, those stories I do tell
To new kids now the dreaded sound, of that fearful school bell.

Eva Corcoran (12)
Ballakermeen High School

A POEM ABOUT CHRISTMAS

I try to get to sleep quickly on Christmas Eve
So it can soon be Christmas Day.
I think about what's going to happen tomorrow,
My family usually come round and stay.

I think about my presents,
I think have I behaved all year.
I think about how many times I've been shouted at,
Oh no I haven't behaved very well, oh dear.

I really can't wait for tomorrow,
Soon Santa will be on his way
With his bright red coat and fat belly,
Only twelve more hours till Christmas Day.

I really hope he'll get down the chimney,
I hope he won't get stuck halfway.
I hope he doesn't land on the coal.
I hope he doesn't land on the cat tray.

I hope he'll be coming down my chimney soon,
I better get to sleep now, I can hear my dad snoring.
I will try and get to sleep now
So it will be soon Christmas morning.

Stephanie Groom (12)
Ballakermeen High School

THE MAGIC GARDEN

I walk into a garden
Which has the magic to pardon,
It has many, many flowers
Of many different powers,
Some birds, some fish,
To eat them is a dish,
But then I notice something strange,
Everything's gone still,
I think I'd better go home,
Back over the hill.
I hope our garden doesn't vanish
For that would be very tragic,
But then I realise something strange,
This garden must be magic!

Luke Simpson (12)
Ballakermeen High School

What Is Magic?

Is magic all about rabbits in hats,
coloured handkerchiefs, wands,
and turning pigeons into bats?

Or is magic about spells and brews,
lizards toes, eyes of newts,
mixed all in a special stew?

Is magic about hexes and charms,
magic potions and curses
that can do terrible harm?

Or is magic about illusions and tricks,
disappearing objects,
and walking through walls made of bricks?

What is magic?

Rachel Grainger (12)
Ballakermeen High School

IF I WAS A MAGICIAN . . .

If I was a magician I'd rule the world,
Everyone would do as they're told.
If I was a magician I'd be top of the class,
All exams there were, I'd always pass.
If I was a magician I'd be the best at everything,
Even playing football on the wing.
If I was a magician I'd put a spell on my sister,
Never again would she have a chance to pester.
If I was a magician I could be anything!

Jamie Smith (12)
Ballakermeen High School

IF I WAS A MAGICIAN!

If I was a magician with all my spells
I'd change my cat who really smells.
I'd do everything with my wand
I'd even conjure up a pond!

If I was a real magician
I'd send my parents on a mission
Across the sea to find gold for me.
I don't think they're that smart
But I'll give them a chance because I'm kind at heart.

If I was a magician with a black cloak
I'd make my friends tell a joke.
I'd give Lisa a brand new coat
To make everyone gloat!
I'd give Sarah loads of money!
Oh that reminds me I've got an empty tummy!

Stephanie Woods (12)
Ballakermeen High School

MY MAGIC POWERS

I have these magic powers
that no one knows about.
I can make rain fall
and stop us having drought.

These magic powers
make me special and great,
they give me the energy
to jump a fire barred gate.

I love these magic powers
so very, very much,
I can do anything I want,
even to speak in double Dutch.

Vicky Radcliffe (12)
Ballakermeen High School

THE SOUNDS OF A COUNTRY NIGHT

The golden sun is about to set
Over the reddy-orange horizon,
But there is still a bit of light yet.

The stars are starting to come into sight
One by one and they're very bright.

The sound of the thrushes
Collecting fruit from the bushes,
Singing their songs as they go
Is one I will never forget.

There's sounds of
The wind that rushes,
Also the river that gushes.

I could hear the hedgehog
Down by the trees.
I could also hear the badgers
Going round in groups of threes.

I could hear the rustle of the leaves
As the fox comes out of its den,
It's probably going to the farmer's
To catch another hen.

Adam Bingham (12)
Ballakermeen High School

IF I WAS A MAGICIAN...

If I was a magician
I would do spells and wishing.
Conjuror, sorcerer,
Enchanter I'll be,
Nobody can ever beat me.

Spells I'll cast
So I'll look back at the past
To see what I did when I was young.
I'll turn people into cats,
Maybe even bats,
Nobody can ever beat me.

So I'll wish and wish
To be like this
But all only
If I was a magician . . .

Katherine Hicks (12)
Ballakermeen High School

THE MIRROR

He stared at it, it stared right back,
He gave the mirror a good old slap.
He looked at it and then he waited,
Getting more and more frustrated.

He went to kick it, it kicked back,
Now his ears were turning black.
'Stop mocking me' he said at once,
The mirror gave the same response.

He looked at it again and again,
Each time he caused a bit more pain,
And then he thought that's my reflection,
Can't you see that's my complexion.

So then he realised all at once
That's why it gave the same response,
And then he gave a mighty shout,
'I'm only five and I worked that out.'

It wasn't anyone at all,
It's just the mirror on the wall.

Barry Maddrell (12)
Ballakermeen High School

CHANGING!

As the autumn mists swirl through the air,
Leaves are falling without a care.

As the leaves change to a golden brown
You know it is altering throughout the town.

As the birds fly away migrating,
The wind will blow with much more hating.

Colder and harsher the weather will be,
Stronger and rougher the sea will be.

You know we've had some autumns, warm with sun,
And you never know this could be the one!

When you think of autumn you think of wind and rain,
But you know two years can never be the same.

Many events take place at this present time,
Like how Guy Fawkes committed that ghastly crime.

So even though the winter is almost here
You can look forward to a happy new year!

Michelle McBride (12)
Ballakermeen High School

A Shot In The Dark

Blood, death fills the air,
The victim's dead but I don't care.
My job is done in a second or two,
He's standing, not knowing what to do.
As he takes his aim I see I'm next
To make an imprint on his chest.
I travel through the air at speed
To go and complete my dirty deed.
When I arrive I feel superior,
Diving into his deep interior.
But now it's all done
And I've had my fun,
I'm stuck in his body, deep inside
And I know his death is my suicide.

John Myers (15)
Ballakermeen High School

SACRIFICE

In a pagan circle,
Sacrifice to Satan.
I see a friend
Being burnt at the stake
To the tune of Sweet Dreams.
Non-believers surround me.
Decay and death fill the air.
Up comes midnight,
I'm now beyond fear.
In front of me
The ground opens,
Up rises the anti-Christ superstar.
My mind is filled with psychotic thoughts,
Suicide, ouija boards, crucifixion,
Perpetual darkness covers the Earth.
Without mounting fear
I realise the horror of my situation,
For I am
A human sacrifice.

David Mercer (16)
Ballakermeen High School

ICE-CREAMS, STRING AND STRONG MEN

I feel like a Magnum on a stick,
or maybe an orange ice lolly.
Either way it hurts when
a little bit more of me melts and falls to the ground,
or when someone takes another bite out of me.

I am the string that holds everyone together,
but yet they are all clawing away at me,
cutting me into little tiny pieces,
until I am no good to anyone.

I see them crumbling under the pressure,
they see me melting in the heat.
And yet they still refuse to put me back in
the freezer and leave me alone to cool down.

I am the strongest man in the world.
I can hold everyone in the palm of my hand,
and still I feel like the weakest person alive.

I am the tasty mint choc chip
that everyone wants to flavour.
But, nobody wants me once they've had a lick,
instead I'm left to melt.

Ouch! It hurts when you fall to the ground.

Kerrie McCauley (15)
Ballakermeen High School

If I Were A Magician

If I were a magician
I would take over the world.
I would put a spell on everyone
To be the most powerful girl!

I would do illusions,
Play tricks on people's brains.
I'd make them see double.
I'd make them go insane!

I would conjure up a spell,
A bit of Hocus Pocus.
I would be so skilful
I would never be out of focus!

I've come to the end of my poem
Of magicians and trickery.
I've taken up fortune telling
Because the future I can see.

Christina Davison (13)
Ballakermeen High School

IF I WAS A MAGICIAN

Abracadabra alla kazam,
Make a sandwich filled with jam.
I will fill a balloon without making it go *boom*,
Then I will sing a funny tune.

I would let the balloon go down,
Then I will turn into a funny clown.
I will never frown
Or let anyone down.

I will always smile,
I will always run a mile.
With my magical feet
I will move with the rhythm of the beat.

Alice Armstrong (12)
Ballakermeen High School

THE SIMPSONS

The Simpsons like to show their bums,
Especially Bart and Homer.
Bart shook up a can of Duff,
And put him in a coma.

Otto is really cool,
He drives his bus into the pool.
Patty and Selma are Marge's sisters,
They always have loads of blisters.

Barney's been a drunk all his life,
He's never had the time to find a wife.
Moe's no better,
He's never had a life.

Flanders is a Charlie Church,
He praises God day and night.
Reverend Lovejoy owns the church,
And always gets a fright.

Semour Skinner owns the school,
No one says he's really cool.
He has a friend who is Scottish,
He's the one who is cool.

Krusty the Clown is a real clown,
He's always clowning around.
Sideshow Mel is a replacement,
For Sideshow Bob who's never around.

Milhouse, Milhouse is a swot
He gets beaten by a clot.
Mr Burns is the richest man in town,
He got shot by a tot.

William Bollen (12)
Ballakermeen High School

WAR POEM

Sirens blasting,
Children crying,
People running to safety,
Bombs lighting up the night sky,
Wishing that it would end.

The sirens stop,
It's all quiet,
Finally it has ended,
People emerge from holes in the ground
To see what damage is done,
But some things you can never replace,
The love, the fear, the hate.

Lindsey Clark (12)
Brae High School

WHAT A WASTE

War machines
Are anything,
Really.

Motorbikes,
Aircrafts,
Cars,
Helicopters,
Is there anything they won't use?
Not even bicycles are safe.
Everything is used and often,
Sent to the junkyard.

Expertly made to
Perfection, they
Get shot out of
The sky or blown off the
Face of the Earth.

Spitfires,
F-16s,
Stealth jets,
They all get blown out of the sky.

British Shermans,
German Panzers,
American M1s,
All get blown off the road.

What a waste,
All those vehicles in a
Scrapyard piled,
Ten high,
Every one rusting away.

David Odie (12)
Brae High School

SNAKE POEM

M any of the mambas will attack on sight,
A rching their back and ready to fight.
M ambas will appear unawares crucifying their
  victims without even a scare.
B e careful of that mamba for it will bite.
A void the mamba at all cost.
S trike from the mamba and a life will be lost.

Michael Manson (13)
Brae High School

SNAKE POEM

S   trike that's what he'll do, strike.

N   o fears, no regrets, he is not afraid
of anything.

A   t night he'll lay awaiting his prey.

K   illing is his means of survival.

E   very creature be aware.

S   talking and striking, he is never fair.

Ross Smith (12)
Brae High School

ETERNAL DARKNESS

I sat in front of the television
Watching the latest war news
Just inches from the front line
Lying still in the damp, muddy trench
I can smell the sweat of the fighting soldiers
And the blood of the men, shot down to their death.
Though the battle carries on
Over the loss of young lives
In a field of ruin and wreckage
Havoc and devastation.

A shiver goes up my spine,
I get closer to my warm rug by the fire
The flames are blazing, heat is pouring out
Bombs are exploding everywhere
Some killing, some hurting
A shout for help no one hears me
The pain is spreading all over my body
Is there anyone there?

My eyes are closing
I yawn with tiredness
I snuggle up to my warm blanket
I lie there waiting for help
I hear footsteps running round me
Voices whispering, 'Is he dead?'
My body floats away into the light
My world fills with eternal darkness.

Nikita Johnson (13)
Brae High School

WASTE OF LIFE

The declaration of war is but a death sentence -
Stealing once innocent lives,
Giving a licence to kill,
To shed blood over earth,
And to poison the minds of young men
Who believe this game to be worth playing.

Ignorant patriots -
Blasted to pieces - dying 'for their country'
Who wait at home, anxious and unknowing,
Of the treacherous inhuman manslaughter,
Committed on bloodstained battlefields.

Children cry for their parents,
Who are lost forever -
How can this bring them a better future?
How do they benefit from this murder?
Perhaps these children will grow to understand,
The utter senselessness of war.

War darkens the blue sky,
Wilts the green trees and blooming flowers,
Fills the seas with blood,
Forces tears to fall.
War makes every step unsafe -
War imprisons you in your own home.

What is the reason for this waste of life?
Introverted men in high places dream,
Of the possible benefits of war,
But did they pause to hear the screams?
Then they may have asked themselves -
What can compensate for life?

Rachael Blyth (12)
Brae High School

WAR MEMORIES

War is a game that shouldn't be about,
Soldiers dying day in and out.
Children who once had a dad,
Can now only look at pictures of when he was a lad.
Wives and girlfriends think and cry,
Wondering why he had to die.
Now he is but a memory,
Not lost but gradually fading away.

Terry Balfour (13)
Brae High School

SHOCKING!

Slowly it slides towards you,
Its slithery body moving closer,
Scary eyes watching you,
It glides past you,
It twists around you,
But still you stand still,
Its poisonous tongue hissing venom,
Sweat running through you,
Suddenly it stops,
Your entire life flashes past you,
Hiss! It strikes you,
Shocking!

Kirsty Thomason (12)
Brae High School

ME, BRITAIN AND WAR

Britain's for war,
War is for Britain,
Ships and planes,
Children's games,
Sensation of soldiers,
Fighting with blood,
Troops on land,
Over hills and sand,
Bombers in the air,
Jerries make it unfair,
Out number us one by one,
Can sometimes be fun.

Shouting and screaming,
Bullet shots beaming,
Jerries are dying,
Their heads are flying,
Crawling between trenches,
Jumping on benches,
We sometimes bet money
With cards - it's funny,
The songs we sing,
In the ear it gives a ring,
Battle at night
When we are nowhere in sight,
Battle in the morning
The Jerries get much warning.

Tanks on the ground,
Army men unfound,
The General's orders
To cross the borders,
Bloodshed is mad,
Stalin thinks it's bad,
I think it's good,
But of course I would,
War is fun,
You get to carry a gun,
A shotgun or a rifle,
It's better than a trifle.

Stuart Milne (13)
Brae High School

WAR POEM

W hen war broke out I hated it,
O ur families went into the war,
R age and hatred flowed through the country,
L oud bombardments all through the night,
D eath toll is very high.

W hen they were lying on the TV about the death toll,
A nd what regiments were hit worst,
R ight then and there I knew Britain was in trouble.

T wice we have been at war with Germany,
W hen the bombardments stopped I knew,
O verall Britain *won*.

Jason Mayes (13)
Brae High School

HOMESICKNESS

H ow I miss my favourite things,
O h my teddies and my bed,
M y TV and my video.
E ddie the elephant and
S am the snake.
I miss my stereo and my PlayStation,
C an I please go home.
K illjoys that's what you are,
N obody really likes you.
E verybody here I go
S o long and
S ee you later.

Sarah Hargreaves (12)
Brae High School

SCHOOL DINNERS

The way the cooks serve it up,
The more I think of spewing up,
The way they make me have some more,
The more they make my tummy sore.

The way I say, 'Oh what a bore,'
When they come with the strawberry galore,
The way the spaghetti moves around on my plate,
The more I think of fish bait.

Oh what a fate.

The way I see the disgusting meal,
The more I think of roasted eel,
Children rush for glasses of water
As they try bits of the smelly slaughter.

The cooks are dirty, nasty and very mean,
I only wish they could be clean,
The teachers think we're being silly and really don't care,
We think it's just not fair.

The way I'm so happy when it's one day to go,
Then the cooks can stop punishing me so,
Oh what a relief, when I smell my mum's roast beef,
My mum's dinners are winners and you've guessed
I was talking about school dinners.

Diana Mowat (11)
Brae High School

HOMESICKNESS

H ow I miss my favourite things
O h my goodness
M ondays mama gave me chocolate bars
E very hour
S undays I got apple pie
I wish I was at home
C ake was one of my favourite things
K eeping in touch was the best
N ever again will I have it
E very minute is agony
S ickness is so horrible
S ickness is so horrible.

Angela Murray (12)
Brae High School

HOMESICKNESS

H ow I miss my favourite things,

O h I'm so homesick,

M ost of all I miss the feel of my family around me.

E njoy? No! I'm so homesick,

S o much I miss my cat,

I ndeed I miss my bed.

C omputers I miss too.

K icking footballs around in the park I miss.

N ever will I be homesick again, it's so bad.

E verybody at home I miss.

S o many feelings I have.

S o homesick.

Christopher Cope (11)
Brae High School

ANGEL WITH GREY HAIR
(For Aunt Jess 1913-1999)

Angels are always thought to be
Golden and sparkling on a Christmas tree.
High in the sky they float around
Sprinkling stardust on the ground.

That doesn't sound like my Aunt Jess
Although she never did make a mess.
Her face was lined with lots of wrinkles,
Her eyes were bright and full of twinkles.

Nature was her very good friend,
It seemed that life could never end.
Yours came to a close at eighty-seven
I really hope you are in heaven.

Send from above your love and care
A real cool angel with grey hair.

Stephen Rocks (11)
Brae High School

SLOWLY DISAPPEARING

Disappearing greenery,
as leaves fall off the trees.
Disappearing happiness,
as plants begin to freeze.
Disappearing wilderness,
as birds begin to migrate.
Disappearing animals,
as they prepare to hibernate.
Disappearing leaves,
bare trees begin to sway.
Disappearing life,
as our whole world fades away.

Nicholas Davidson (12)
Brae High School

HOMESICKNESS

H ow I miss my favourite things,
O h how terrible homesickness is.
M y sisters always make me laugh
E ven when I'm not that nice.
S ometimes I feel really ill,
I never get to sleep at night.
C oming back home was the best,
K eeping away was always the worst.
N ow I never go away.
E very hour goes so slow.
S ometimes I just want to cry.
S ometimes I just want to go home.

Jenna Johnson (11)
Brae High School

HOMESICKNESS

H ow I miss my favourite things
O h I miss my family
M ostly the animals, mam, dad and my scrambler,
E lderly old granny
S itting in that house
I also miss my favourite friends
C hecking I am, all the mail to see if there's any for me
K icking the wall if there's none
N ext week there might be something
E nough I said to myself
S end me something to eat
S end me something to tell me that you're alright.

Peter Robertson (12)
Brae High School

WAKE ME WHEN IT'S THE WEEKEND

Wake me when it's the weekend,
Let me sleep, I don't want to get up,
To take a shower and put on my uniform
At six thirty, then run for the bus.

Wake me up when it's the weekend,
Then there are no tests, lessons or homework.
Let me play, sleep, daydream, watch TV and play sport.
So . . .
Wake me when it's the weekend.

Vincent McAviney (11)
De La Salle College

STRESSED OUT

My first few weeks
At senior school
I felt really stressed out,
So many books and things to carry.

Will I ever survive?

So many classes, so many teachers,
What am I going to do?
But then I said to myself,
'What is there really to worry about?'

I'm very organised and that's a fact,
Timetable sorted, classes found.
Teachers are nice, which I think is sound,
No more stress, senior school is the best.

Brendan Roberts (11)
De La Salle College

RULER OF THE REMOTE

I am the ruler of the remote,
I lay as if I'm on a boat,
I won't let anyone have the remote
                        from five till nine,
What can I say, it is not a crime.

I like to hold the VCR remote too,
Because my mum and dad don't have a clue.
I like the Discovery channel on sky,
To watch the birds fly high.
I nearly forgot I have also got to be
The closest to the TV.

Sean Kenny (11)
De La Salle College

WAKE ME WHEN IT'S THE WEEKEND

On Monday morn
I woke with a yawn.
'Your first day at school today.'
I then woke with a scream,
What a terrible dream
I hope I don't have that again.

On Tuesday morn
I woke before dawn,
All hot and sticky in bed.
I had a dream
In which I had seen
Myself all withered and dead.

On Wednesday morn
I heard a car horn,
'Jonny, five minutes till school.'
I got out of bed,
Bumped my head
And fell down upon the floor.

On Thursday morn
I woke with a yawn
And it suddenly dawned upon me
I was in my dad's bed
With a cracking sore head
And a lovely hot cup of tea.

On Friday morn
I woke with a yawn
Feeling all happy and bright.
I got out of bed
Off fell my head
And I've never had such a big fright.

Jonathan Poole (11)
De La Salle College

BAD HAIR DAY

Every single morning of every single day
I wake up to find that the gorilla came to play!
I go towards the cupboard to get out the gel,
Now, that got my hair down very well.

Rory Harman (11)
De La Salle College

COMPLETELY MENTAL

I am mad, I am crazy,
I am anything you want me to be,
My face is green, my tone is mean,
And I am a Jersey bean.
My eyes are yellow, my voice is mellow,
But I say don't go mad go mental.

James Warley (12)
De La Salle College

WAKE ME WHEN IT IS THE WEEKEND

Monday morning, 7 o'clock,
I wish I could fall back with a loud flop!
Please would you wake me when it is the weekend?
Will you? Will you?

Why oh why must I wake up?
I know I will say I have a contagious cut!
Please answer my question
When it is the weekend!

It is time to go to school,
I feel like a tired fool,
Again,
Wake me when it is the weekend.

There is no escape in anything I try,
Oh if only I could fly,
Please, please, please
Wake me when it is the weekend.

Tom Whiteley (11)
De La Salle College

STRESSED OUT

I'm stressed out!
What shall I do?
I've got loads of homework,
Oh poo.
Right David, calm down, relax,
Me relax, that will be the day,
Shall I go to the doctors to see what's wrong?
Nah, they won't do anything and nor will my mum.

David Gaffney (12)
De La Salle College

IMAGINE

Imagine all the people
Crying and dying.
Imagine all the children
Crying out for their
Mums and dads.

What would we have tomorrow
If the world ended today?
We want to live in heaven,
But yet, we still dwell in hell.

Declan Varian (13)
De La Salle College

IMAGINE!

Imagine all the people
Wandering around the world,
Seeking for something to do.
Imagine no animals
And no religion too.

Imagine there's no food,
Hunger and poverty reigned,
It's pretty hard to do.
Imagine all the people
Living for today,
All around the world.
People may say you are strange
But you don't really care.

Jason Olver (13)
De La Salle College

ASSUME

Assume that there's no
Heaven, no hell
And no beliefs.

Assume that there's no
Killing, no war,
The suffering is over,
Death a thing of the past,
And there are no weapons,
Not one in whole wide world.

Assume the world is one,
No different cultures,
No different religions,
The world united,
No need for war,
The brotherhood of man.

Assume that there's no
Rules, no strict laws,
No need for punishment,
One world, one culture,
One religion, the world as one,
The culture of the world.

Luke Palmer (14)
De La Salle College

NOTHING

Nothing to kill or die for,
Nothing to live or cry for,
Nothing to jump or laugh for,
Nothing at all.

No need for greed and hunger,
No need for poverty and anger,
No need for death and slaughter,
No need for anything at all.

Imagine there's no people,
Imagine there's no countries,
Imagine there's no world,
Imagine there's nothing at all.

Harley Woodward (13)
De La Salle College

IMAGINE

Imagine there's no transport
And no road, rail or sea,
We would be stuck all on our own
With other people to be.

Imagine there was a life outside ours
In the far, far galaxies
Where other little people were going to work
And shopping, driving and learning,
Just like us.

Imagine we could breathe under water,
Imagine there were underwater towns
And you could speak and hear under water.
What would you say?

Edward Cookson (13)
De La Salle College

NO HELL BELOW US
(Inspired by John Lennon)

Freedom for you and me,
No hell below, nowhere for me to go,
So where do I go when I'm picked to die?
I'll have to go up high.
Will I be greeted with open arms,
Or sent to live behind bars?

So what do I do while waiting?
Waiting to die!
Do I choose a life of crime or a life of
                            happiness and love?
The second option is what I choose,
Or will fate choose for me to live and die
                                        alone?

Live life to the full, is what I hear,
What is the 'full'?
But how will I know when I have done it all?
Will I have a happiness that will fulfil,
Or will I pass it on some idle Sunday?

Nicholas Hogan (13)
De La Salle College

WHO WILL PAY?

Look at the world today,
Suffering, dying, withering away,
The world is falling to evil,
The battle is over and very much won,
The loser is now suffering,
But in the end, who will pay?

The earth is dying, but who does care?
No one is bothering to answer its prayer.
There is so much we could do,
But do we bother?
No, not at all.
Living life in luxury,
We don't give a damn.

Soon this Earth will be in disrepair,
Too hot and baked by the sun,
The consequences we will clearly see
As a result of our life of fun.
When all we had to do was try a little harder,
When all we did was sit there
And did absolutely nowt.
So at the end of the day,
Who will pay?

Hugh Thomas (13)
De La Salle College

IMAGINE YOU CAN FLY

Imagine there's no hell,
Imagine everybody can fly away,
To where they want to go.
I have lived for that very day,
To see everybody fly away.

I can see the Earth under my wings,
Maybe some day everybody
Will be able to fly away,
High into the sky,
Leaving the planet far behind.
Maybe some day you'll join us too,
High in the skies.

Just try to imagine just for one day,
It's not all that hard
To imagine to fly away.

Neil Cotillard (13)
De La Salle College

WORLD PEACE

The world is suffering,
People killing for no reason,
Killing for greed.
They should realise there's no need.

People dying needlessly,
Thousands every day,
In cold-blooded murder
And they think it's okay.

Why does it always have to happen,
Why do nations have to fight?
Why can there never be world peace?
That would just be right.

Paul Williams (13)
De La Salle College

THE FUTURE

What will happen in the future?
Will robots and technology be the end of us
Or will we be the end of ourselves?
What will happen?
The way we rely on machines so much, it scares me.
One day when machines and technology are so
                                  important,
And they fail to work,
What will happen?
Will the world come to a standstill,
Or will we just start to fight among ourselves?
If we do,
We'll probably launch so many nuclear bombs
That we'll blow Earth to pieces,
That is my biggest fear.

Brian Henderson (13)
Mid Yell Junior High School

CARS

All the tiny nuts and bolts
the wheels and metal
make the car go rumble.

You fuel it up
then fire it up,
then the car goes
clatter, bang, clik,clak.

You jump in, then fire it up,
toot, toot.
Going full speed zooming through the roads,
then the car goes thundering on.

Then the car goes beep, beep,
it's out of fuel.
Oh botheration.

Marcus Nisbet (12)
Mid Yell Junior High School

VOICE OF THE FUTURE

The world has changed,
It's no longer peaceful,
The cars go by with noise and pollution,
And they use up too much fuel.

The world has changed,
It's no longer pleasant,
The grass has turned brown,
And the animals are disappearing.

The world has changed,
It's no longer untroubled,
War plagues the world,
And the threat of destruction strikes
                    fear into humanity.

The world has changed,
It's no longer tranquil,
Cities keep on growing
And the people in the cities rush
                    to meet deadlines.

Matthew Simpson (13)
Mid Yell Junior High School

TARANTULAS

Tarantulas are hairy, ugly things,
patrolling the area as they run
with their hairy legs scurrying along.
Tarantulas, little evil things with
poisonous teeth and poisonous hairs,
ready to spring out at unsuspecting prey.

Brendan Scollay (13)
Mid Yell Junior High School

WHAT LIFE IS ABOUT

When I lie in bed and think,
My past springs into mind,
I think about all the friends I've lost,
In and out of time.

When you get older,
You begin to realise
That life is too short
For friends to fall out,
'Cause in the end, you'll need them.

When I was younger,
My sister and I always fell out.
Now we're older we get along
And both know what life is about.

Martha Clark (12)
Mid Yell Junior High School

A POEM ABOUT FAMILIES

Families are a
gather of people.
A mixture of adults
and children.

Families are loving,
they love you like
you are their teddy bears.
They comfort you when
you are upset.

Families are serious.
Some families are funny.
My sister and my mother
argue all the time.
It's not nice when that
                    happens.

Families may hate you,
but deep down inside,
they really do love you.
You are a part of them,
just like a petal is of a flower.

Hayley Nisbet (13)
Mid Yell Junior High School

The Mud Race

In the mud-drenched hills
The power and speed thrills
Of racing a quad or a trike.
The race is on, the engines revving.
The smell of petrol, the wheels,
The mud spraying.
The victory, I'm praying,
Is mine as I go through a rut . . .
On through a hole, the muddy wheels churn.
The rival is now abreast on the winning straight,
We race for the best.
I'm gaining and then . . .
I feel the power surge through the quad
As the front wheels lift in a victory wheelie.

Vincent Tonner (13)
Mid Yell Junior High School

THALIDOMIDE

When I'm older,
I want to be a
rally driver,
Formula 1 driver,
touring car driver,
cab driver,
but I can't.
The doctor gave my mum
Thalidomide,
this drug ruined my life.
I was born disabled,
I have to go about in a
wheelchair.
I will never drive,
I will never have fun.

Mark Odie (12)
Mid Yell Junior High School

BATTERY HENS

We are in a cage
with no space to move,
we're in a confined world.

I wonder how you would feel
in an enclosed world?
There is no shining sun,
space to do nothing,
I'll never see the sun or the grass.

I see nothing,
so much still to be seen.
It makes me unhappy
to know I'll never see sunlight
and wide open spaces,
endless amounts of land.

Lee Jamieson (12)
Mid Yell Junior High School

SOMEDAY

I see children running around weeping.
I see men, covered in blood.
The whole town is coming to an end!
Day by day the gruesome sights get worse.
I don't understand why the governments
put their countries through so much grief!
                    Bang!
There goes someone else's life.
This place isn't safe anymore!
Mines are planted everywhere!
Someday this world will come to peace,
someday soon this world will come to rest!

Carly Gray (13)
Mid Yell Junior High School

NOT WANTED

Stuck in a cage
all alone, nowhere to go
and nothing to see but the
metal bars of a rusty cage.

I face other dogs dying,
the vet coming
sadly
to tell the owners
that the dog is better to be
put down.

I wish I was not a stray.
I've waited from last year's April
to this year's May,
but still no one wants me.
I wish I was not alive.

Belinda Anderson (12)
Mid Yell Junior High School

TURTLES AT SEA

The people alive in the world today,
Think that turtles come out for their prey,
The evolution of themselves they really don't know,
So every year out of the sea they flow,
Walking home not very fast,
Tallying each year as they go past.

People never know why their shells are so tough,
But my opinion is that the sea can get rough.
Turtles know of course they have it just in case,
Animals try to eat them, but still they're safe.
Turtles, they really love their shells
And rattle their heads inside them like bells.

People think turtles are hardly ever seen,
Because they don't like the colour of themselves green.
Is it on what they feed
Or do they get stuck in the seaweed?
Which one is it I really can't find,
If it's the one on food I really don't mind.

Turtles move very slowly indeed,
Maybe because they're fat on greed.
I'm not sure if they like being slow,
But I think they do, as they've got a flow.
People say turtles are easy to beat,
But maybe not if they've got two extra feet.

Many species of turtle are known to you,
But maybe I can only think of two.
The people from China think there are four,
But the people from Africa think eight or more.
Australians think there are one or two,
But the Americans think just a few.

Wrecked ships in the sea,
Is the worst place for a turtle to be.
In the sea you get no sun,
So I don't think it would be much fun.

Claire Furner (10)
Murray's Road Junior School

TO THE LAND OF THE FREE

I would love to be a horse,
all free in a field,
galloping with my friends,
till the sunrise dawns.

I would be called Silver Star,
splashing in the waves,
I'd canter on the beach
to my heart's content.

I would nuzzle the children
and jump elegantly,
then carry them bare back
to the land of the free.

Demelza Le Ber (13)
The Grammar School, Guernsey

THE CHANNEL ISLAND HIKE

The time has come after practising and preparing
To face the challenge ahead.
There are teams from Guernsey and Jersey too,
Of three to help you through.
Activities are first aid, compass work and
Communication.
They all include teamwork, leadership and skill.
We camp overnight and cook too,
With stoves and gas with lots of small pans.
At the end of the day we came fifth
And
Learnt a lot of stuff
We didn't know before.

Charlotte Harris (13)
The Grammar School, Guernsey

FAR OVER THE MISTY MOUNTAINS COLD

Far over the misty mountains cold
Lies a legend of magic untold
Where an evil wizard who no one can name,
Brought despair, destruction, grief and pain.

He filled every heart with hate and dread,
He killed imagination dead.
The flowers died and the birds passed away
To find a longed-for brighter day.

Marching over the misty mountains cold,
To solve the legend of magic untold.
We've got to try and make a start
To mend the broken, bleeding hearts.

Elaine Higgins (13)
The Grammar School, Guernsey

THE BOX

It is said to rule lives,
The people just watch it day and night,
It doesn't respond to you,
All it does is have moving pictures.

How come we love it?
We must see more of it,
And catch up on what happened.
Did he die or did he live?

Are we obsessed with this box?
How come it grabs our attention?
Why is it so important to us?
After all, it is only a box.

Is it a health hazard?
Does it stop us doing important things?
Does it ruin our lives?
How much harm can one magic box do?

Catherine Dimelow (14)
The Grammar School, Guernsey

MY ALIEN FRIEND

The other day I went for a ride,
How I got there, I can't decide.
My mum thinks that it's just pretend,
But I really did meet an alien friend.

Up, up, up and away I go,
Where I'm going nobody knows.
If I told you, you wouldn't believe me,
Unless he comes down here to see me.

Next time I go I'll invite him down,
He'll come to my house and I'll show him round.
Then if he likes it he can stay,
I'll ask him when I go on Monday.

My mum said it's in my head,
But now he sleeps at the end of my bed.

Lucy Potter (13)
The Grammar School, Guernsey

THE DAFFODILS

I never think of clouds as being lonely,
I never think of sadness being blue,
I've never seen bluebirds beyond the rainbow,
I don't believe the Bible is all true.

But daffodils do dance upon the hillside,
I've seen the sun make diamonds out of dew,
I've seen the world is all aglow at sunset,
I believe at dawn each life can start anew.

Merrilees Harris (13)
The Grammar School, Guernsey

A DREAM OF SUCCESS

Every Saturday I have a dream
Of playing for the world's greatest team.

Before the match we grab to eat
A pastie full of veg and meat.

Shouting and screaming from my seat,
My skin boiling from the sun's heat.

The game starts, we all jump up,
Hoping at the end of the day the league reads United top.

Then I dream of how it might be,
If everyone came to watch me.

The ball is pumped up the park,
Hoping I can make my mark.

I control the ball and have a run
And play it to the winger, who takes his man on.

With power and pace he whips in the ball,
To his annoyance, nobody's in the box at all.

The ball rolls back to me to their dismay
I then take a touch and tuck it away.

The fans go ecstatic and sing aloud,
While I go and celebrate to the crowd.

I hear the crowd shouting as I awaken,
To see Yorke slot the ball home for a goal well taken.

I hope one day this dream comes true,
But for dreams to happen it's down to you.

Darren Martin (13)
The Grammar School, Guernsey

BUNTY

I think that the tortoiseshell cat
Who lives with my gran
Is a sly old thing.
Her slit green eyes have seen
Glass mountains,
Emerald caves
And the outer rims of space.
She is on the prowl,
Alert, yet calm.
My gran calls her back,
Bunty runs home
To play with her string,
And sleep in front of the fire.

Laura Kelly (13)
The Grammar School, Guernsey

THE GOOD LIFE

Calling for this, calling for that,
She's got better things to do than sit on a mat,
Eat, drink, sleep all day,
She doesn't even have to pay!
Shop for her, take her to the vet,
Why do all this when she's just a pet?

But at night it's a different story,
She doesn't see us with such glory.
We pick her up and stroke her head,
When she'd rather be tucked up in her bed.
Out into the dark and cold she goes,
She feels the frost beneath her toes.

She has to fend for herself 'til morning.
Lucky she doesn't find it boring,
Off to find a mouse,
She'll bring it as a present to the people in the house.

Morning comes once again,
She returns to the house with a hunger pain,
She receives strokes, hugs and a good morning smile,
She's been waiting for her food for quite a while,
Eventually it comes and she's so happy,
She digs in; it's not at all scrappy.

But suddenly she hears a shout,
Mum's seen the mouse no doubt,
Back to her basket she goes
And washes herself from head to toes,
She curls up in a ball,
And falls asleep, she's tired after all.

It must be easy just doing that,
Sometimes I wish I was a cat.

Sian Jones (13)
The Grammar School, Guernsey

MANCHESTER UNITED

Gary Neville,
What a star,
He's not just brilliant,
He's the best by far.

Brother Phil,
Pretty good,
What a prospect,
All this young blood.

Thanks United
For all you do,
My life's like a dream
And it's down to you.

Keep it up
As long as you can
Because I will always be a loyal fan.

Sam Jones (13)
The Grammar School, Guernsey

THE DOG THAT SAT UNDER MY CHAIR

There was a dog
That sat under my chair,
He was so quiet,
I hardly knew he was there.
He had very deep brown,
Puppy dog eyes
That made him look
Like he could tell no lies.
He was wearing a coat
That was as black as night
With socks on his feet
That were clean and white.
His tail was wagging
Back and forth
His body giving off
A friendly warmth.
He looked up at my face
With a long but gentle gaze,
But he then ran away
Without even a glance,
Just one clear bark,
Lingered in the dark
To show that there
Had ever been
A dog that was sitting
Under my chair.

Laura Elder (13)
The Grammar School, Guernsey

IS HALLOWE'EN WHAT IT SEEMS?

Hallowe'en comes but once a year,
Kids dress up not for your fear,
But purely for chocolate, money and sweets,
Trick or treat down their nearby streets.
Ghosts, ghouls, goblins they are,
Dressed in sheets they look bizarre,
'Trick or treat,' they scream,
Give them sweets, their faces beam,
All this in the means of fun,
But something stirs long after the sun.

Midnight, the witching hour,
Witches gather with great inner power,
Demons growl by their side,
Had this superstition not died?
Lightning crackles in the distance,
With no thundering assistance,
'Hubble, bubble, toil and trouble,
Bring forth evil and make it double.'
The witches turn and flee,
In case a human was to see.

Men, women and children fall down dead,
Slowly but surely the plague does spread,
The violence moves from town to town,
Knocking all the living, breathing down,
Not just humans but animals too,
Out in the wild or in the zoo,
Eventually the world is no more,
All is gone but the witches' gore,
So on October the 31st beware,
Cos if the witches gather in their lair . . .

Jon Langlois (13)
The Grammar School, Guernsey

SOMEWHERE TO NOWHERE

The dusty roads led to nowhere
With deserted houses on either side.
Noises sounded in the distance,
Noises unknown to mankind

That fade and disappear.
No one to disturb the
Peacefulness or tranquillity
Of the devastated town.

The deserted houses in ruins,
Blanketed in cobwebs
And ivy, and the debris
Of a panicked departure.

The dusty roads led to nowhere,
With deserted houses on either side.
The volcanic clouds hung over the town,
Changing it from somewhere to nowhere.

Ellen Le Huray (14)
The Grammar School, Guernsey

GOING BACK

I walked the uneven riverbank
Stumbling beside the black, angled stream
The glassy water wore a transfer
Of streaky sky and sooted chimneys
Oozing their thick, gaseous poison
I met with the road.

The leaves rustled, chattered and fluttered
In crumbling piles and whispering heaps
And levitated above the pavement
A penetrating silence descended
Like a black mist, rank with fear
I shivered.

I strode on with slow, purposeful steps
The world smudging and merging around me
The wind roared silently through the bare branches
I considered their sharp, spiky form
I turned the corner of 55 Avenue
I stopped.

I had reached my destination
The bone-hard, smooth and sharp-angled steps
Screamed out and cut into the thick atmosphere
The Chapel Steps held their evil secret
Their sickening, heart-gripping truth
I knew.

A fierce gust of wind snatched my hair
Warning me away, blowing me to safety
Just as my head clockworked and spiralled
Why did I come, why did I come?
I turned from the Chapel Steps, from 55 Avenue
I never went back.

Laura Taylor (14)
The Grammar School, Guernsey

MIRRORS

I look to the mirror
See the image on the wall
Staring at me.
Looking where I look,
Seeing what I see.

Bewildered emotions,
Glorious happiness,
Solemn sadness.

How it frightens me
To see that reflection,
Reflecting my life to all who look.

Light rays shine, dance into my eyes,
Block out the image which confronts me.
Then it is dark, I cannot see,
But the reflection still shines back at me.
Crystal detail, perfectly sharp.
How I look, how I stare.

And then I move,
Is my reflection still there?

John Murphy (14)
The Grammar School, Guernsey

CLOUDS

They fly above the sky,
Covering the Earth with their
                    thick blanket.
Sometimes they're black,
Sometimes they're white,
Yet they fill you with wonder,
Why are they there?
What's their purpose?

Flash! As the light fills the sky,
The clouds rage with curses and
                    bright lights.
The storm passes, leaving a dark monster
Slowly moving away.

Iain Scott (14)
The Grammar School, Guernsey

THE COMMON COLD

Monday morning's come.
You've just got up for school,
You realise you're not well
And feel just like a fool.

Your nose begins to run,
Your throat is dry and sore,
Your tissue box is empty
And the remote is on the floor.

Your CD player's jammed,
Hot water bottle's cold,
Chocolate is forbidden,
Get well is all you're told.

They've just had weekly art,
You're getting in a huff,
You've missed your TV show,
It's awful and it's rough.

Your temperature has soared,
You think you've got the 'flu,
Your best mate's mum just rang,
Now Sheila's got it too.

Next morning you feel better,
The cover's nice and soft,
But Dad starts making noises,
Just working in the loft.

I do not like the sneezes,
I hate it in your head,
The best bit though is this,
Your breakfast in your bed.

Natalie Henry (14)
The Grammar School, Guernsey

THE KNIGHT OF SHINING DEEP

There came a knight of the Shining Deep,
And he did ride with righteous blade
That cleaved the land, his light was shorn,
His sword of might aloft was borne,
So all could see his glorious stroke,
'I shall never fall,' his strong voice spoke,
But when time came, he felt to leave,
He left the lands of evil foe.
His self to rest in ancient deeps,
Where none can conquer peaceful sleeps.
And that today is where he lies,
Sits watching and helps us in our lives.
He is the knight of Shining Deep
Who rides to battle on phantom steed.
The gates swing wide for he who'd pledge
This knight has blade of mithral sovereign edge,
To burn the land with redemption's fire.
He is the lord, the Shining Deep sire.

Nick Bougourd (14)
The Grammar School, Guernsey

LOVE

Love swoops and glides and flies at night,
love's wings are gold and creamy white.
So soft and gentle, a wondrous thing,
as magical as a diamond ring.

Love comes but once to all of us,
just wait for love, it will not rush.
One man, one woman, they come together
but who knows, will they stay forever?

Love is one mysterious creature,
it's good, it's bad, it is a teacher.
Pure, blissful love is just a tale
and after a time, it soon goes stale.

Love drops and thumps and stomps at night,
love's wings are black and grey, so right.
So heavy and rough, a dangerous thing,
as off-putting as the cats that sing.

Rachel Webb (14)
The Grammar School, Guernsey

THE HEART OF HEARTS

This feeling in hearts
when lovers' eyes merge into one,
as soul secrets are brought to tongues,
and inseparable pairs thought as one.

A war of the self begins,
the human heart will always win
for purely one reason it will concur,
the aura in which it carries, is love.

Finding a heart that
in which a feeling of fire burns,
is destiny's task as it is the heart,
the heart of us all.

Laura Wadley (14)
The Grammar School, Guernsey

THE STORM

The wind whipped up the trees
In the very strong gale force breeze.
At night the sky was set alight,
With the lightning and it gave us a fright,
Slicing the sky in two.

After the lightning, there was set for something
To be even more frightening,
The thunder that made a big bang.
The rain gave my sister a scare,
It was so loud she could hear it coming up the stair.

The waves got churned up as if it was
in a washing machine.
Then the mountains of sea spray would
Pound against the sea wall and land on
                                passing cars.

Ben Brouard (14)
The Grammar School, Guernsey

THE MASSACRE

The low-toned hum
That echoes through your mouth,
Scrubbing and spinning,
Whirling about.

The twisting head flicks
At a tremendous pace,
To devour anything
That's out of place.

Splatters of white sludge,
Flick about,
The murderous machine
Leaves nothing out.

Then the button is pressed,
The carnage is over.
A deadly hush . . .
The electric toothbrush.

Tim Nicolle (14)
The Grammar School, Guernsey

RIVERS

Trickling gracefully out of the Earth,
Pure voice, the beginning of tides,
Joined by another, now mutually set
Onwards, ever onwards they ride.

Down through the valley, under the trees,
Oceans answer the call.
Silken and shimmered, glittered with gold;
Laughing, united they fall.

Now overflowing, in currents drawn closer,
The end of the wanderings cease.
Flashing in sunlight, they race for their home
Out from the warland to peace.

Finally weary, they seep through the sands
Into the depth of the blue.
Their mission completed, their journey fulfilled;
One with the wave and the moon.

Jessica Sharp (14)
The Grammar School, Guernsey

MONDAYS

The bell of my alarm clock rings,
I awake and think of the joy Monday brings.
I get up and crawl to the bathroom,
Where even a shower won't suppress my doom.

I pack my bag with all I need,
For instance, my kit for the lesson of PE.
I put on my clothes and wander downstairs,
Where I take out a brush and straighten my hair.

Once at school (or prison to you and I)
I do my lessons where I really do try.
Later that day, I go home and reflect,
Maybe it wasn't so bad,
Though there's room for improvement yet.

Gemma Barnes (15)
The Grammar School, Guernsey

GET OVER IT!

I can hate you more
Than you can hate me
You are the person
Who just can't see
That messing us about
Can only lead to trouble
So you'd better watch out
Protect your bubble.

You've treated us all badly
For such a long time
It's now time to show you
We are just fine.
We don't need you
To be in our lives,
We know that unlike you
We can always strive.

We know what's right,
We know what's best
So go away and
Join the rest.
You are so worthless
You know us not well,
Leave us alone
Before we reach a really bad spell.

Anon (14)
The Grammar School, Guernsey